at home with
COLOR
WAVERLY®

Meredith® Books
Des Moines, Iowa

Meredith® Press
An imprint of Meredith® Books

WAVERLY® AT HOME WITH COLOR

Editor: Vicki Ingham
Project Manager: Lisa Kingsley
Art Director: Marisa Dirks
Copy Chief: Terri Fredrickson
Managers, Book Production: Pam Kvitne, Marjorie J. Schenkelberg
Contributing Copy Editor: Jane Woychick
Contributing Proofreaders: Nancy Dietz, Beth Lastine, Nancy Ruhling
Photographer: Jeff McNamara
Indexer: Elizabeth Parsons
Electronic Production Coordinator: Paula Forest
Editorial and Design Assistants: Kaye Chabot, Mary Lee Gavin, Karen Schirm

Meredith® Books
Editor in Chief: James D. Blume
Design Director: Matt Strelecki
Managing Editor: Gregory H. Kayko
Executive Decorating and Home Design Editor: Denise L. Caringer

Director, Retail Sales and Marketing: Terry Unsworth
Director, Sales, Special Markets: Rita McMullen
Director, Sales, Premiums: Michael A. Peterson
Director, Sales, Retail: Tom Wierzbicki
Director, Book Marketing: Brad Elmitt
Director, Operations: George A. Susral
Director, Production: Douglas M. Johnston

Vice President, General Manager: Jamie L. Martin

Meredith Publishing Group
President, Publishing Group: Stephen M. Lacy
Vice President, Finance and Administration: Max Runciman

Meredith Corporation
Chairman and Chief Executive Officer: William T. Kerr

Chairman of the Executive Committee: E. T. Meredith III

WAVERLY®

President: Christiane Michaels
Vice President, Marketing & Licensing: Carolyn D'Angelo
Design Director of Licensed Product: Christina Angelides
Design Director and Stylist: Kristin Osterberg

The editors of *Waverly® At Home with Color* are dedicated to providing you with information and ideas to enhance your home. We welcome your comments and suggestions. Write to us at: Meredith Books, Decorating and Home Design Editorial Department, 1716 Locust St., Des Moines, IA 50309-3023.

To find the location of a Waverly retailer near you, call 800/423-5881. Or visit our website at www.waverly.com

Waverly is a registered trademark of F. Schumacher & Co.

Manufactured and distributed by Meredith Corporation. If you would like to purchase copies of any of our books, check wherever quality books are sold. Or visit us at meredithbooks.com

Cover photograph: Jeff McNamara

Trend watchers may be saying that color is back, but for Waverly, color never went away. The hues of the natural world—of spring, of the sky, of earthy spices and sparkling jewels—have never ceased inspiring our designers to create beautiful things for your home. The goal of *At Home with Color* is to give you color confidence so you can make your home beautiful and comfortable. Many people, feeling unsure about committing to color, fill their homes with shades of beige—and that is wonderful if the Naturals and Neutrals palette is for you (see page 28). But there is a whole world of color out there and a perfect fit for every personality—even a Natural palette can be spiced up with a dash of color. Color can energize, enlighten, calm, or inspire. *At Home with Color* will make you a color expert in your own home; it will give you guidelines on the use of color without dictating what is right for you. It will show you how to apply this knowledge using our extensive selection of fabrics, paint, wallpaper, furnishings, and accessories. So have a cup of tea, settle into your favorite chair, and soak up all of the vibrant, dreamy, restful, and romantic possibilities of color.

Happy decorating!

Christiane Michaels

Christiane Michaels
President, Waverly

"The purest and most thoughtful minds are

table of contents

those which love colour the most."

—— JOHN RUSKIN, *The Stones of Venice*

how to use this book

So you're ready to try your hand at domestic artistry and paint the canvas of your home with the perfect palette—but where to start?

A good place to start thinking about color choices for your home could be a personal preference—a hue you simply love and feel comfortable with. Maybe it makes you feel serene or happy or energized or simply at home. Perhaps it is the color of a favorite flower or the dominant tone of your favorite season.

Another approach is to take a color that is an element in a beloved quilt, rug, painting, or chair and extrapolate from that a scheme for a room or for your whole house. Sometimes you have a preestablished color that you need to work around, such as a tiled fireplace surround or colored fixtures in a bathroom. (Houses of the 1920s to 1950s, for instance, often featured tile, tubs, sinks, and toilets in shades of lilac, pink, or pale blue-green.)

You might take a cue from period architecture in your home. That doesn't mean you have to restore it authentically, but you might find inspiration in the period colors to help you devise a color scheme that suits you, your home, and today's color palettes.

Consider, too, the function of a particular room. High-use rooms, such as kitchens and family rooms, are best done in soft, easy colors that are livable day in and day out. Less-frequently used rooms can take stronger, more saturated color. A formal dining room, for instance, may be painted in a shade of passionate crimson.

The first section of this book, Learning About Color, introduces you to the basics of color theory—how different colors work together and the effect they have on an environment—and helps you determine what kind of decorating personality you have. The second section, Living with Color, puts that theory to work by showcasing beautifully appointed rooms that employ Waverly's spectrum of palettes: Naturals and Neutrals, Crimson, Jewel, Spring, Sky, Spice, and Whites.

You'll get ideas for filling your home with color, choosing a decorating style that suits your personality, arranging furniture, and accessorizing your home.

naturals & neutrals

crimson

LEARNING A

jewel

Without a doubt, you have a favorite color or colors— hues that make you feel good. But you might wonder how you can apply those colors in decorating your home or how they work with other colors. What follows is a brief exploration of color theory that will help you understand the relationships among colors, the effect particular colors and color schemes have on a space, and the way colors make you feel.

spring

sky

BOUT COLOR

spice

whites

get primed with a lesson in color

■ The color wheel offers a simple, visual way to understand the relationships between colors; it can help you put colors together for pleasing effects in your home. A review of lessons you learned in science and art class helps explain how color works.

White light is made up of every color in the rainbow: red, orange, yellow, green, blue, indigo, and violet. When it passes through a prism, white light separates into individual colors because each color has a different wavelength. Red has the longest wavelength and violet the shortest. We perceive a certain object as green because the surface of the object absorbs all but the green light waves, which are then reflected back to our eyes.

Now for the art part: The color wheel—an array of the colors of the spectrum—shows how colors relate to one another. Color relationships are key to no-fail color schemes. Colors that are next to each other on the color wheel are referred to as analogous. Because one is an element of another, they are harmonious. Their contrast is subtle.

Colors that lie opposite each other on the color wheel are complementary. Because they don't share common elements, they are in high contrast. Complementary colors intensify each other.

PRIMARY, SECONDARY, TERTIARY COLORS

Red, yellow, and blue are the three primary colors. They are called primary because they cannot be mixed from any other colors. Theoretically, any hue in the infinite color universe can be made from the three primaries, plus white and black.

Orange, green, and violet are the secondary colors. They are made by combining the primary colors. Combining equal parts of a primary and secondary color produces the tertiary or intermediate colors. In a standard 12-segment color wheel, the intermediate colors are named by joining their parent colors with a hyphen (for example, yellow-orange, and so on). With each successive blending, the colors become softer and more subtle. Even if it is unlikely you will be mixing your own paints, having a grasp of these color concepts will make choosing colors for your home much easier and will ensure that you love the results.

BLACK, WHITE, TONES, AND NEUTRALS

Technically, black and white are not colors, but they are used to make shades and tints of colors. Tone is a term that refers to how dark or light a color is. Adding black darkens a color's tone and creates a shade of the original. Adding white lightens color tone and creates a tint. (Pastels start with white and are made by tinting it with other colors.) When working with more than one color in an interior space, it is wise to use colors of similar tone.

Neutrals are so named because they do not side with particular colors on the color wheel; they can serve as a backdrop for nearly any kind of color scheme. Neutrals can be warm or cool; they also can constitute an entire color scheme by themselves.

Colors generally are referred to as either warm or cool. Red, orange, and yellow radiate warmth and energize the room and its inhabitants; blue, green, and violet cool things down. They create a quieter, more serene atmosphere than their hotter counterparts. Even a cool color, however, can have warm overtones.

warm

Green, for instance, is made from a warm color (yellow) and a cool color (blue). If it tends to the yellow side of the spectrum, it will appear to be a warm green, and vice versa.

To the eye, warm colors advance; they make something seem closer than it actually is. Cool colors recede; they make an object appear farther away than it actually is. Think of how red flowers seem closer than the green foliage that surrounds them. This principle is important to keep in mind when you are choosing a wall color, whether you plan to paint the wall or cover it with wallpaper. If you have a very large room that you want to warm up and make feel intimate, consider a vibrant red or yellow; if you have a small room that you wish felt bigger, consider painting it a pale blue or a light neutral. To square up a long, narrow room, paint the end wall a warm color.

cool

LEARNING ABOUT COLOR SCHEMES

■ A monochromatic color scheme is a one (mono)-color (chromatic) scheme. It is based on just one color but employs variations of that color by adding white or black or by adding a touch of that color's complement. Three different tones of a color is a workable number to use in a monochromatic color scheme. You need deep-colored areas, mid-tones, and highlights. A bedroom could be done in shades or tints of blue, for instance, with creamy white as an accent. The higher the contrast between the tones, the more energy you create in a room; the more subtle the gradations in the tones, the more subdued the mood of the room becomes.

monochromatic

LEARNING ABOUT COLOR SCHEMES

Neighboring or analogous colors flow from one to another; they are closely related and generally look harmonious together because the eye easily runs between them without abrupt transition. Wide ranges of lightness, darkness, and intensity of color can be used in an analogous scheme because the colors are so closely related. The intensity of the colors and the contrast between their tones determine the mood of the room, making it feel calm or kinetic. As in a complementary scheme, choose one dominant color—blue, for example—and use its neighbor, green, as an accent color.

analogous

Any three colors that are equally distant from one another on the color wheel (so they make an equilateral triangle) form what is called a triadic color scheme. As in other color schemes, choose one dominant color and use the other two as accents. This allows one color to set the mood of the room so the viewer can experience the ambience with one sweeping glance. When one color sets the stage, the room has a visual anchor and the space will not appear busy or chaotic. With a triadic scheme, you can alter the mood of a room by switching the dominance between the warm and the cool color.

triadic

■ Perhaps the most popular color scheme is one color plus white. The color provides the visual interest; it makes a room feel warm or cool, expansive or intimate. The white defines and accentuates the qualities of that color. Here, white makes citrus tones appear crisper and warmer than they would be standing alone.

1 color + white

A complementary scheme covers all of the color bases. Complementary colors lie directly across from each other on the color wheel; literally, a complement is that which makes perfect. Every pair of complementary colors has a warm and a cool hue. The two colors intensify each other but also create a natural balance.

complementary colors

■ The appeal of white is its serenity, purity, and simplicity. When decorating with white, the key to a feeling of warmth is to use a mix of whites.

Using just one tone of white can make a room feel sterile; combining warm and cool whites in a variety of textures, patterns, and materials imparts a sense of depth. Texture has heightened importance when you are decorating solely with whites, because the way light falls on different surfaces affects how color is perceived. Shiny surfaces such as porcelain, for example, reflect light easily and make whites appear brilliant and bright, whereas matte or textured surfaces absorb light and make the different tones of white seem softer and more subdued.

white on white

at home with color

We may not be conscious of it, but our eyes seek a balance of color in our environment. A leafy green plant soothes the senses in a warm-colored room; a burst of red from a bouquet of roses or tulips warms a cool one.

Although creating a balance of color in a room is not an exact science, you must first think about whether you want to base your color choices on a monochromatic, complementary, analogous, or triadic scheme. After that, you must decide how much of each color you want to use. In general, one color dominates a room and the other (or others) is used as an accent. You can also use equal amounts of two or three colors. This creates a high-contrast room that is visually stimulating.

balancing color

What's your personal style? Read on to find yourself in one of Waverly's decorating personalities. Use the profile to guide your color and decorating choices as you create beauty and comfort in your home.

LEARNING ABOUT COLOR
decorating personalities

past perfect You are a romantic who loves vintage furnishings and accessories, such as Grandmother's china, old quilts, and garden-inspired textiles. You like elements of American country, Victorian, and Scandinavian style. Comfort is key; if you don't have a cottage in the woods, you create one where you live. You like weatherworn textures and soft colors. For you, antiques shops and flea markets are like honey to a bee—and nothing is sweeter than that perfect find from the past.

town & country

You embrace both environments suggested by the name of the style: the sophistication of historical motifs drawn from art and architecture, luxurious fabrics, and rich colors—and simple, clean lines that aren't fussy or frilly. You like a balance between formal and casual elements and are able to blend a rare piece of sculpture with a gilt-framed "Sunday painting" by an amateur artist. The seamless result is classic elegance and comfort.

beautiful things

Everyone loves beautiful things, but you value gracious living and timeless, traditional looks. That means you surround yourself with 18th-century-style English and French classics wrought in rich woods. The English garden inspires your decorating choices—floral-motif wallpapers, fabrics, needlepoint pillows, and botanical prints. Your favorite accessories might be your collection of Blue Willow china or Staffordshire dog figurines.

modern living

You like airy and spacious rooms but still value a sense of warmth, which you achieve with graphic checks, stripes, and whimsical prints. Although you don't want to be overwhelmed by pattern and clutter, intriguing furnishings and accessories contribute to the visual interest in your home. A yard sale find sits next to a sentimental accessory or piece of furniture. You like a fresh, lighthearted style that's contemporary and transitional; you want your home to charm guests into a smile.

colors of provence

You've read *A Year in Provence* by Peter Mayle at least twice, and you travel to the south of France and other European locales via your imagination as often as possible. European and Indian-motif cotton fabrics are the hallmark of this style. These attract you with their exotic beauty and their casual comfort. You love vibrant, warm, saturated colors and French and Italian country furniture in rustic pine and distressed walnut.

naturals & neutrals

crimson

L I V I N G   W

jewel

Now that you are well-versed in color concepts, it is time to get down to the tangibles: living with color, whether that involves lounging, playing, cooking, or sleeping. On the following pages is a gallery of real-life rooms decorated in seven fresh, livable palettes. Use the rooms to guide and inspire your own color choices. Regardless of your decorating style, you will find beautiful color combinations that suit you.

spring

sky

TH COLOR

spice

whites

WP311
Clotted Cream

W

at home with
NATURALS
& NEUTRALS

"All art is but imitation of nature."

—LUCIUS ANNAEUS SENECA, *Epistles*

naturals & neutrals

What could be more comfortable than an interior that echoes the great outdoors with the colors of the earth itself? Naturals and neutrals exist in their purest form in desert sand, seashells and driftwood on the beach, and stone cliffs above the sea. They are found on the farm in lamb's wool, straw, cornhusks, and a glowing field of wheat. In the farmhouse, they are reflected in the hues of buttermilk biscuits, heart-of-pine floors, a well-worn pair of khakis, or a wicker rocker on a sunporch. On the pale side of the palette are shades of ivory, bone, and cream. Neutrals with tinges of gray include taupe, mushroom, and stone. Even certain shades of olive green are considered members of this color family. Darker colors of this palette include a range of browns, from coffee to cocoa. Naturals and neutrals are beloved for interiors because they are comfortable and understated, elegant but not ostentatious. Their simplicity makes them perhaps the most versatile of the color families. Manifested in a sea-grass or sisal rug and raw-linen curtains, they are casual and earthy. Add a cashmere throw or a piece of classical sculpture, and the palette takes on a sophisticated air. In large, solid swaths, these colors are timeless and classic. In eye-catching prints, they are as interesting as the most saturated palette. They can make up a whole color scheme or act as a subtle background for more vividly hued furnishings. Like a soul whose patience is endless, whose presence is soothing, and whose disposition is serene, the family of naturals and neutrals is easy to live with and easy to love.

same colors
different styles

MODERN LIVING

Everyone is seeking simplicity, it seems, but no one wants to sacrifice style. Modern Living achieves that goal, with uncomplicated but sophisticated style. Expressed in a comfortable neutral palette, this approach is especially useful in giving a modest space a roomy feel, whether in an urban apartment or a small room in a suburban home. In this apartment, starting with white walls and a light neutral color scheme enlarges the perception of space. Neutral colors in interior design became popular in the 1920s, when Germany's Bauhaus School of Architecture and Art stressed functionalism and clean, uncluttered lines in its designs. Much of what we now call classic contemporary style—or Modern Living—has its beginnings in Bauhaus designs. It is natural, therefore, that the Modern Living style is so comfortable in neutral colors. The light neutrals on the walls, floor, and furnishings reflect the ample sunlight that streams in the balcony doors. The raw-linen draperies that frame the doors soften the space, and accessories of natural woven wicker add warmth and texture.

Classic contemporary style is defined by clean lines,
uncluttered spaces, and earthy but elegant neutrals.

opposite Angular furniture crafted in blond wood is a hallmark of classic contemporary style. Here, a blond-wood credenza serves as a neutrally toned anchor in the dining area. A row of simple picture frames of different sizes, flanked by lean 1950s-style lamps, align along their bottom edges to provide a pleasing parallel line. Other embellishments for the top of the credenza could include mid-20th-century wood or ceramic sculptures, or broad, shallow African-style woven baskets.

right Interior designers often define a neutral as a color that can be used as a backdrop for other colors and textures. You need only step outside to see that green fits this description. Glossy deep-green bowls and the greenery in the row of topiaries pick up the subtle sage green in the palm-print fabric of the napkins and slipcovers. Although the scene may strike you as "green" upon first glance, it is still decidedly neutral, thanks in large part to the natural motif of the botanical-print fabric.

left Every space, and perhaps an urban-style space most of all, needs some earthy elements to keep its inhabitants in touch with the natural world. This nubby linenlike fabric, printed with an airy palm-tree motif, is botanical rather than floral, which keeps its style in line with a clean, uncluttered look.

Accent colors in a neutral scheme? Here's how:

Employing a neutral color scheme does not mean your home has to be devoid of color. A fair amount of green (albeit a soft, subdued green) appears in the neutral family, which means that pulling out an accent color is easy and appropriate. There are two ways to do this. You can use a deeper shade of the same color, for a monochromatic effect, or you can use a subdued, browned- or grayed-down shade of its complement (in this case, red). The soft green in the palm-tree print and striped tablecloth, *above left*, gets a boost from a deeper shade of green in the porcelain bowls and in the cording tied around the napkin. The same effect could be achieved with beige and brown, or gray and black. A scalloped salad plate in a warm tone of terra-cotta red, *above right*, serves as a complementary accent to the sage green in the napkin. When you pair an accent color with its complement, keep the tones (intensities of light and dark) of the colors similar so they look harmonious together.

opposite In a small space, each piece of furniture and every accessory must be carefully considered and chosen for its form as well as its function. The dining chairs in this apartment, for instance, serve multiple purposes: for convivial meals with guests, of course, and for comfortable seating and after-dinner conversation as well. Slipcovers open the possibilities for a change of pattern or color when the scene or the season changes. The chairs could be dressed in another print in an even subtler or deeper shade of sage green, or in a textured solid in a tone of green, cream, beige, or soft brown.

The soft, tea-stained hues of neutrals are a natural
choice for lovers of the vintage, cottage look.

same colors
different styles

PAST PERFECT

The Naturals and Neutrals palette can be used in any decorating style, and the Past Perfect decorating personality is well-suited to nearly any color palette. Clearly, however, these two are meant to be together, as this country kitchen demonstrates with casual ease. The soft, tea-stained hues in the gingham window shade and tablecloth suggest a homespun character. The pine ladder-back chairs with rush seats and the accessories—taupe-colored crockery, hand-thrown pottery, and a well-worn wooden dough bowl—bring natural materials into play and contribute to the vintage atmosphere. For a change of pace, the large-check gingham tablecloth could be switched to another old-fashioned print, such as a nostalgic floral or petite stripe; the solid table skirt acts as a color anchor.

make neutrals exciting

You like the comfort and user-friendliness of neutrals but still want your home to be visually interesting. A word to the wise: Remember the infinite possibilities offered by pattern, texture, and motif. Khaki-colored walls and camel-colored sofas set this living room firmly in a neutral scheme, and natural motifs and lots of interesting patterns and textures make it a pleasant, well-designed space. Accessories, including a tiger pillow, an eye-catching zebra-print footstool, and a bamboo tray table filled with potted orchids, impart a touch of the exotic. A nubby sisal rug creates a broad stroke of texture underfoot; throw pillows in plaid and draperies in a bold stripe add pattern.

left Furnishings in neutral colors and natural materials mix well together even if they are of different styles. A rustic armoire of knotty pine, for example, pairs well with a more formal side chair, thanks to the casual look of the caned seat. A well-designed space invites lounging, so keep lots of pillows on hand. The coordinating linear patterns of these pillows give life to the corner, while a dragonfly pillow underscores the natural motif.

opposite The walls in this room, as well as the most dominant pieces of furniture, are covered in solid colors. If you want more texture and pattern in your own neutral scheme, consider using a textured wallcovering, such as grass cloth, or upholstery in patterns or prints.

right Inject a breath of the outdoors into the living room by arranging an aromatic herb garden planted in mottled clay pots on the mantel. In choosing accessories, look for items that will work with the color scheme and the decorating theme or motif of the room. Here, the terra-cotta pots reinforce the nature theme.

create richness and drama with neutrals and white

Although intrinsically subtle, neutrals can be rich and dramatic with the judicious use of white as an accent color. White accents make any color—even the muted green walls in this restful bedroom—seem deeper in tone because they create contrast. The deeper a color's tone, the more drama the contrast has. (For the same reason, photographs and pieces of art, such as those on the mantel and wall, are best framed by white or light-colored mats.) Architectural features that are painted white, such as the wood trim, door, and fireplace surround, lend the room definition and a crisp, clean look. In fact, architectural trim—crown molding, cornices, baseboards, and so on—is the one place where pure, brilliant white is visually effective (on walls and other broad areas it creates too much glare). Remember, white comes in many different shades; if you prefer a softer effect, tint the white trim color with a bit of your wall color.

make more space
and light with neutrals

You want the space where you greet the day—the place you go before you have your first cup of coffee—to be full of light. This small bathroom needed brightening and a boost in its sense of space. A neutral palette was the only logical choice to accomplish both goals without sacrificing the natural style of the room. Painting a paneled portion of wall white and curtaining the shower with a linen-and-white plaid helped visually enlarge the room. The light colors also reflect the rays of sun that stream in the window. Without these touches of white, the light would be absorbed by the dark tones of the wood and tile. The use of neutrals keeps the color scheme harmonious, almost monochromatic.

enliven
neutral walls wi
artful paper

Neutral color schemes may be easy to live with (and safe from a resale perspective), but they don't have to be ho-hum. In the palm-tree print kitchen, left, and in the garden-inspired dining room, right, wallpaper in neutral colors creates instant art for the walls. In a kitchen, where cabinetry lines the walls and dominates the room, wallpaper provides pattern and visual interest to balance the cupboards. In the dining room, a tone-on-tone paper supplies a subtle, space-enhancing effect, while the border above the chair rail accents the room's architectural features. The topiary-print border also corresponds thematically to the pressed fern fronds displayed in the frames above the buffet. Framed pieces show to best effect against wallpaper when the print or artwork is surrounded by a wide white or cream mat.

break up
the monotony

ou like neutrals, but an expanse of off-white walls doesn't quite have the visual impact you'd like. The answer? Divide your walls and apply a combination of wallpapers or paints in the same color family. Almost all neutrals work together beautifully, so creating a combination of color and pattern (or patterns) that looks cohesive is a fail-safe proposition. (One tip: Choose either warm or cool neutrals—not both.) Three different patterns appear between the sunroom and the hallway, *opposite*, but neutrals link the two spaces. In the bathroom, *right*, a narrow shelf serves as a functional and decorative element. Its position provides a visual break between the wallpaper and the paint, which look lovely together in their easygoing neutral tones.

at home with
CRIMSON

"Getting bored with red . . . would be like

crimson

In languages throughout the world, the word for red has its roots in the word for blood. Red is the color of the pulse of life itself; it represents the essence of us all. In nature, red is the color of attraction: the red male cardinal vies for the attention of the female; red flowers draw hummingbirds to feed. Red invokes the strongest human emotions, from the fever of romantic love to the fury of war. Exposure to red causes human respiration and pulse rate to rise. Sense of smell becomes more acute; taste buds become more sensitive; appetites are piqued. In a red dining room, we may indulge more—and experience the food as far more tantalizing—than in a room of any other color. The lusciousness of ripe strawberries, raspberries, cherries, and pomegranates is undeniable, but hunger is not the only appetite aroused by red. Red is the color of passion, the

getting bored with the person you love."

—— DIANA VREELAND, *fashion editor and designer*

tint of lips and cheeks flushed with excitement. Red is dramatic and not terribly subtle. Marc Antony could not have misunderstood Cleopatra's intentions when, having prepared a romantic dinner for him, she had the floor covered with crimson roses 18 inches deep. Despite its primal implications, red is also elegant and luxurious—like a velvet pillow or a glass of good port. It is the color of power and not retreat, but it does make a room into a retreat, a place that feels, above all, secure and warm.

crimson

same colors
different styles
TOWN & COUNTRY

If you love the elegance of a little black dress but crave the comfort of your blue jeans, the Town & Country style fits you to a tee. Rich color is one of the signatures of this seamless melding of formal and casual styles. And few hues have more brilliance and versatility than crimson does. The pillows on the bench, *left*, present a microcosm of how seemingly divergent patterns and styles work together. The floral is formal and the plaid casual, but they are of the same tone of red. The dining chairs, *above* and *opposite*, provide another example of how color can marry seemingly opposite styles. The white cottage-style chairs are casual, and the slipcovers are crisp and tailored; a classic red and white toile brings the two styles into harmony.

crimson

same colors
different styles
BEAUTIFUL THINGS

Want to be swept off your feet? If your ideal evening is one spent lingering over a romantic candlelight repast, make a dinner date in a room whose vibrant crimson walls hold you in a passionate embrace. Beautiful Things style is for the romantic traditionalist. Nothing could be more romantic than the intensely warm, saturated red in this dining room. In keeping with Beautiful Things style, English garden florals soften the sweep of solid color in the window treatments, the rug, and the botanical prints. Rich-looking, dark wood dining chairs have round backs—cleverly echoed in the display of red and white transferware plates—that impart a certain femininity to the room.

above Red is a dining room classic for a good reason. Red stimulates the appetite, and light—especially lamplight and candlelight—intensifies the color's warmth, so the room positively glows. A well-lighted red room is flattering to its occupants, making crimson the perfect color for spaces that are used for entertaining.

crimson

opposite The subtle repetition of shapes, colors, and patterns creates a sense of symmetry in this room. Floral-print place mats with a solid overlay repeat the striking combination of floral drapes and solid-color walls. White Italian ceramic accessories add a touch of romance and create shapely silhouettes against the crimson walls and dark wood table. Place mats allow the beautiful wood to show; for a more formal look, a solid white tablecloth could be used with crimson chargers, crystal stemware, and red and white dinnerware.

above If you already have enough drama in your life, you might want a softer, less color-intensive effect. The solid-to-print ratio in this room could be reversed, with floral wallpaper and solid-color drapes. Or, for a subtler change, simply upholster the chairs in a print.

crimson

cozy up
with crimson

S pace is nice, but wide expanses are not very intimate or cozy. To make a large room warm and inviting, divide it into smaller areas. Then turn each area into a cozy conversation spot by filling it with soft upholstered pieces, plenty of pillows, and interesting accessories. Crimson, a naturally warm color, advances from any surface it covers, making the distance between the crimson object and the viewer seem smaller than it really is. In this rustic living room, two sofas face each other; the upholstered benches between them invite you to put up your feet and settle in with a good book or a good friend. A vivid Turkish-style rug warms up the space and ties all of the smaller areas of the room together.

left Simple tab-top draperies in a crimson-and-cream stripe filter the light, bathing the room in a warm glow. This glow may not make the room seem smaller in scale, but it certainly imbues the space with a sense of comfort and coziness. White walls and an expanse of windows allow the room's fifth surface, the floor, to play a key role in establishing the room's color personality with a vibrant Turkish-style medallion rug. A line of red bowls on the window ledge creates a visual boundary to the room.

Warm colors like

left A rustic trunk-turned-bench transforms a space under the stairs into a cozy spot for reading, contemplation, or simply sitting. A box cushion and billowy pillows in a mix of vibrant prints and solids soften the surface and create comfort. Framed art on the wall above the bench defines the intimate nook as an area of interest and function in its own right.

rimson advance, closing the gap between objects—or people.

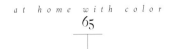

There is a beautiful simplicity in using just one color to decorate a room, particularly if you are passionate about that color and do not want to dilute its impact in any way. A monochromatic color scheme can be as rich and visually interesting as any multiple-color scheme if you do three things: use a range of tones in that color; incorporate a balance of solids and prints; and apply pattern generously. A variety of reds warms this bedroom, from the soft, tomato soup red of one pillow to the ruby red of a pair nearby. A mix of patterns is used fearlessly: in plaid curtains, bed skirt, and lampshade; vertical-striped pillows; a paisley-and-damask-striped pillow; and a floral duvet. You won't significantly depart from a monochromatic color scheme by mixing in a bit of a neutral for visual relief, as was done here with the khaki and red striped bed pillows.

one color
lots of interest

enhancing architecture

Color can enhance the architectural features of a room, such as the dramatic arch in this entryway. If a room lacks structural interest, color can create some. Here, the red toile fabric wallcovering creates a background foil for the arch, and the elegantly carved wood frame enlivens the print. In a room lacking such structural features, white trim against solid-colored walls is a classic way to add interest. In more contemporary settings, the trim and walls may be painted in a monochromatic scheme or in similar tones of complementary or analogous colors. Even furnishings can take on an architectural role when a solid-color piece with a defined shape—such as these white dining chairs with round backs—is set against a background saturated with color.

crimson

Even the most ardent fans of red admit that their favorite fiery hue could use a little cooling down now and then. To cool crimson, soften the tone and toss in a cool accent color in a similarly subdued hue. The kitchen, *opposite*, is a deep salmon-red. The accent color of the cabinet stain is a fellow primary—blue—but it's a soft, pewterlike expression of the color rather than a pure, clear azure. In the entryway, *right*, the wallpaper is a browned-down brick red. The accent color, green, is its complement and appears in the vase and chair fabric. Again, it's a subdued, grayed version of the color, almost a verdigris (the patina copper takes on after years of exposure to the elements), not a Kelly or lime green. The earthy, organic hues are harmonious and balance the color and sense of temperature in the rooms without extinguishing the fire.

cool the fire...a little

at home with

JEWEL

"Look, how the floor of heaven is thick

jewel

Like the plates of precious metal called patines that were used for ceremonial purposes during Shakespeare's day, the Earth's plates hold things of beauty: brilliant gemstones prized for their color, rarity, and lore. Jewel tones can be muted, as in the deep, dusty purple of ripening grapes or plums, but more often they are expressed as bright, pure, clear, saturated hues: amethyst, magenta, lapis, and greens that range from emerald to jade to malachite and turquoise—with an occasional burst of golden topaz. Historically, the jewel palette has been the realm of the bold and the passionate: rulers, religious figures, and artists. To be "born to the purple" meant you were of royal blood. Caesar proclaimed purple to be for the exclusive use of the emperor. During his rule in Europe, Napoleon decreed a deep, bright green as Empire green and lavished it on his state apartments. Artists have always been attracted to the drama of the jewel palette. An intense blue paint made from lapis was

inlaid with patines of bright gold."

——WILLIAM SHAKESPEARE, *The Merchant of Venice*

a prominent element in the luminous color schemes of the Renaissance. In the early 1900s, when the Russian Ballet was all the rage in Paris, the regal, jewel-like colors of Imperial Russia were splashed all over the interiors of upper-echelon Europe. The palette imparts a touch of the exotic, appearing in Turkish carpets, pink Peruvian and brilliant blue Incan textiles, and the delicate, incandescent magenta silks and embroidered, sequined fabrics of India and the Far East. Whether they are used in small bits or in broad sweeps, jewel tones have a bold and regal bearing that is anything but boring.

same colors
different styles

MODERN LIVING

F eeling dull? Here is the antidote: bold, graphic Modern Living style executed in dynamic jewel tones. This eye-catching living room reflects an artist's sense of color and shape and an unerring design confidence. Some pick a palette for their home by choosing from the colors associated with its architecture; others flout those conventions with great flair, as was done in this Arts and Crafts-style home. A scheme of muted greens might be more in line with a period palette—but there are no rules mandating historical accuracy in decorating your home. This Modern Living space fuses vibrant colors and bold shapes with timeworn accessories such as the earthenware jugs and weathered stool, both of which add texture and warmth to the room.

jewel

left If you are ever in doubt about which colors go together, look to nature—specifically, flowers—for inspiration. Fresh flowers in shades of fuchsia, magenta, and canary yellow capture in miniature a vivid jewel palette that accents and enlivens the dominant bold blue note of the room. Flowers make excellent accessories for underscoring a room's color theme, and they breathe life into the setting better than almost anything else can. When the blooms fade, have on hand accessories in like tones: cranberry glass or yellow ceramics, for instance, or a mosaic table, bowl, or vase inlaid with bright glass beads or colorful pottery shards. For an additional burst of color, consider setting accessories atop a hand-painted tray, a folk art table rug, or a shawl or table scarf woven in lapis blue, citrine yellow, or bright ruby red.

Jewel tones impart a touch of the exotic to any room.

above Solid colors are often brought into traditionally furnished rooms
as rest for the eye from pattern. Here, the opposite occurs: A brilliantly
hued and intricately patterned Turkish rug breaks up the monotony of
solid blocks of color and gives the room the allure of a faraway land. The
rug also allows design flexibility in the future; its colors could blend into
almost any decorating style.

jewel

The subdued side of the jewel palette is perfect for expressing the sophisticated, refined air of the Town & Country style. The palette and the style draw on historical motifs from art and architecture, as exemplified by the Italian style of this living room. With the exception of the voluptuous, ruby red pillows on the sofa, the jewel tones take on a soft patina that allows the Della Robbia-style fireplace to be the centerpiece of the room. The Renaissance-style painting of the monk and the gilt-framed art on the mantel suggest the appearance of timeworn but luminous Italian frescoes. The creamy white walls create a blank canvas from which the art and the subtle jewel palette truly shine.

same colors
different styles
TOWN & COUNTRY

On the stack of books:

MICHELE CASCELLA | ETRUSCULUDENS

Louis Agassiz Fuertes & the singular beauty of birds   Harper & Row

ROLLING STONE · THE PHOTOGRAPHS

left It's the little things that count. In asserting a soft palette in a predominantly white room, each accessory must be carefully chosen for how it amplifies the color palette and the style of the primary furnishings. Here, a reddish-plum pillow, a purple candle, and a bouquet of purple heather stylishly do the job. Because the hues of the pieces are soft and muted, they don't appear abrupt to the eye in this airy environment; they enhance the stunning architecture of the fireplace instead of competing with it.

opposite The upholstery on the chair picks up the color in the classic Italian fruit-motif print draperies. For a slightly more dramatic look, the chair could be covered in a dusty plum or deep, muted yellow. The Italian country-style side table is the epitome of Town & Country: a comfortable blend of refinement and rusticity. The table is refined in its form but turned out in rustic, distressed pine.

Regardless of their depth or brightness, analogous colors (those that are next to each other on the color wheel) are fairly subtle side by side in a stripe—as they appear here—because one is an element of the other. A striped fabric in an analogous scheme with an even application of each color is highly versatile. The overall look of this loft decked out in azure and jade, for instance, can be weighted toward green or blue, depending on how the room is accessorized. Primarily blue pillows that take center stage and cobalt blue dinnerware make it a blue room with green accents. That could easily be reversed with the green pillows in front and green dishes on the table.

creating balance
with analogous colors

Exuberant jewel tones are a delightful choice for a child's room. To make the space restful rather than energetic, limit the strong colors to the fabrics. Slipcovered headboards, duvet covers, draperies, and pillows create the color personality in this room and can easily be changed as the child's preferences change. The color principle at work is that the dominant color, violet-blue, is what is called an intermediate or tertiary color. It is made by mixing a primary color, blue, with a secondary color, violet, blue's color wheel neighbor. The accent colors, green (analogous to blue) and shades of red and pink (analogous to violet) are from the same side of the color wheel. The close relationship between all the colors makes the differences between them subtle, so the result is restful, despite the vivid hues.

creating harmony
with multiple colors

jewel

right It is said that the divine is in the details. Certainly in decorating any room, it is the little extras that refine and finesse the look and feel of the space. In a room decorated with multiple colors, there is ample opportunity to pull out individual colors in the palette for such details. Instead of hidden buttons on this duvet cover, pink ties are employed. They put the fun in functional, serving as an embellishment and a closure.

left Pink piping made of the same material as the duvet ties defines and flatters the edge of the cover, preventing it from looking flat. The ties and piping follow the simple decorating principle of repetition; each one strengthens the presence of the other. Individually, they might be lost to the eye.

left Velvety, plum-colored draperies are held back by a simple tasseled gold cord that picks up on just a hint of yellow in the duvet cover. The easily untied cord and weighty fabric are perfect choices for a child's room, where streaming sunlight can interfere with afternoon naps and summer bedtimes.

opposite Slipcovered headboards in beautiful blue punch up the color in this room. Pretty and practical, they are easily removed for cleaning—a must in a child's room—and may be replaced with another color, depending on the season or your need for a new look.

If Michelangelo had stuck to the notion that a ceiling had to be white, the world would be decidedly poorer for it. Traditionally most ceilings are white (largely to make them appear higher), but there is no rule that they have to be devoid of color. In fact, in homes with high ceilings, a canopy of color makes a room seem cozier. Either paint or wallpaper may be used to top off a room with color. In the red dining room, *opposite,* a simple geometric wallpaper on the walls allows the ceiling to feature a sumptuous floral paper without overwhelming the room. A linear floral border introduces the random floral on the ceiling and serves as a visual transition. In the living room, *right,* sapphire blue paint was applied to the ceiling. The draperies and lampshade echo the color; all three of these elements connect in a pleasing triangular symmetry and enhance the paisley-stripe paper on the walls.

create a canopy of color

at home with
SPRING

"Come, gentle spring! ethereal

spring

How often, in the midst of winter, have you wished for an eternal spring? Although you might not get nature to cooperate, you can envelop the interior of your home with the freshness of spring all year long by filling your rooms with shades of green, soft pink, and touches of yellow. Fittingly, the word "green" comes from the same root word as "grow." The fertility of nature is evident in the green of soft, velvety moss; a sunlit meadow; a mound of glossy limes. Each year when winter wanes, this verdant canvas is punctuated with pink peonies, azaleas, and tulips, and yellow buttercups and daffodils. Green is a blend of passive blue and active yellow; it is the color of harmony and balance. Scholar Pliny the Elder opined that green delights the eye without tiring it. Green induces a feeling of tranquillity and meditation. You can't help but feel good in green surroundings;

mildness, come. "

—— JAMES THOMSON, *The Seasons*

add green's complement, pink, and you will look good too. Pink makes the skin radiant. In Indian folklore, the beautiful women of the harem danced by the light of the full moon in gossamer pink gowns. In the 1950s, Audrey Hepburn popularized pink taffeta, and soon the color was in the closets—and all over the walls—of homes across the country. During that same decade, Madame Ritz had all of the lampshades in her Paris hotel lined with pink fabric. The flattering glow emanating from the lamps inspired her guests to return again and again—just as spring does so faithfully each year.

same colors
different styles
PAST PERFECT

If you have always dreamed of having a little rose-covered cottage in the woods but the practical matters of life have prevented it, bring the cottage home to your house. In this restful living room, the soft pinks and greens of the spring palette are naturally expressed in florals that recall an English cottage garden. The muted green walls and subtle striped sofa provide a background that echoes the verdant foliage of the garden; the scattering of soft pink and yellow roses in the fabric suggests endless blooms. A coral pink chaise longue with curving arms and a box-pleated skirt is feminine without being frilly—a lovely place to put up your feet and sip a cup of tea.

spring

same colors
different styles
MODERN LIVING

Pink is not the sole province of little girls, cotton candy makers, and hopeless romantics. If you like the softness of pink but find that a little goes a long way, you can incorporate it into your home and still maintain a simple, sophisticated look. In this Modern Living art studio, the salmon color in the sofa and chair slipcovers provides a touch of softness, a muted expression of pink in clean, linear patterns. Despite a floral throw pillow or two, classic contemporary furnishings, such as the laminate-top table of blond wood, fix this space firmly in the Modern Living style.

Salmon and apricot are sophisticated expressions of pink.

spring

start fresh every day

Mother Nature has to wait a whole year to start anew, but you get a chance every morning. Reading the newspaper and nibbling a croissant in a dining room cast in the colors of spring is a lovely way to wake up. The soft, analogous palette of this room takes its inspiration from a field of daffodils. Yellow- and green-painted walls sit side by side, just as these colors do on the color wheel; color placement depends on the source of light in the room. The room's fifth surface, the floor, also provides a canvas on which to splash color. Note that the yellow and ivy-patterned rug is large enough to accommodate the table and chairs comfortably, even when the chairs are pulled out.

opposite The lighthearted feel of this room is achieved by its color scheme and its motifs, which support each other beautifully: yellow and green plaid draperies; a buffet embellished with a spring bouquet; and porcelain tulip plates. A slightly different combination of elements could have the same fresh effect: The wall with the French doors could be papered with a floral or garden-motif wallcovering, for instance, and paired with solid-green drapes and rug, as well as solid-color painted furniture.

right The Italian-style fruit-embossed plates make terrific basic tableware for this room. Here, the ivy-rimmed bread plate picks up the ivy-and-trellis motif in the rug. The yellow and white plates could be used with different glassware and accessory plates or bowls— perhaps with a touch of pink— to achieve a whole new look.

Look to Mother Nature for inspiration

When you are working with an analogous color scheme (as in this dining room) or a complementary scheme, use different intensities of each color to keep the scheme interesting. Each tone of one color should correspond to a similar tone of the other color or colors. To understand this concept, look to nature, where there are no color mistakes: Light and dark green plants live side by side, as do flowers of varying shades of pink or yellow. In the photos, *above,* the stem and bloom of a pink tulip sum up the spring palette in a complementary scheme. A topiary-style bowl of moss (whisked away when lunch is served!) is part of an analogous scheme of yellow and green.

Every day is a spring day when it starts out in a dining room awash in sunlight and blooming with fresh color.

The question of what he said and what she said is answered in this bedroom—they both love it. This spacious room is airy and enveloping, romantic and contemporary. A blend of furnishing styles, light and dark woods, and masculine and feminine touches, the room is perfectly cohesive because color ties everything together. The walls are painted a nostalgic, whisper-soft yellow, and because they are largely unadorned, the eye is drawn to the sunny yellow chair in clean-lined, classic contemporary style. Every square foot of your home does not have to be covered with color to have impact; sometimes one burst of color is just the thing to provide optimum visual interest. Here, the intense color of the chair provides radiant warmth in a small dose. Despite divergent styles, the chair and the painted yellow European country-style bureau make a compatible pair. The color and the style of the bureau are in keeping with the floral-print comforter and the ruffled, unabashedly feminine pillows that accent it. The effect is not a result of design indecision, but a blending of styles that is at once soft and simple.

tie your styles
with color

Bathrooms should sparkle. To that end, most of them are outfitted with white fixtures and hard surfaces, such as ceramic tile, that are moisture-resistant and easy to keep clean. But these practical choices can create a sterile-looking, hard-edged space that is not very inviting. In this bathroom, the green towels, rug, and shower curtain soften the white and neutral tile and walls. Warm green (one with plenty of yellow) is a good color to use in a bathroom because it visually cushions a space while imbuing it with freshness. Green is clean. Color is not the only thing working to dull the edges in the room. The foliage-print shower curtain adds the lushness of fern fronds, a motif repeated in the pressed-leaf pictures.

soften a hard space with color

Like its namesake season, the spring palette can be cool and restful (think of a lush green garden on an overcast day) or sunny and sprightly, depending on which color or colors are used. A bedroom, *left*, is the picture of repose in cool, monochromatic green. The strong presence of white in the coverlet and wispy curtains adds to the dreamy ambience of the room. Of course, you want your bedroom to be restful; but a touch of energizing color isn't such a bad idea when the alarm clock rings and it is time to face the day. Balanced doses of the warm colors of spring—soft pink and glowing buttercup yellow—imbue a different bedroom, *opposite*, and a living room, *below*, with just the right amount of energy.

soothing spring,
sunny spring

spring

To make your home appear more spacious and cohesive, apply the basic visual principle of using the same palette throughout the house, unifying the rooms with color. If you happen to love the soft, feminine hues of spring, fear not: Pink and green can be grown-up and sophisticated and are applicable in any room. This dining room, *opposite*, and bedroom, *left*, employ white as the main color. Pink and green are added in sparing amounts and in airy patterns that don't overwhelm the space. In the dining room, tailored slipcovers of the palest green are in perfect keeping with the formal, Italian-style dining set. In the bedroom, muted expressions of pink and green—as well as sophisticated touches such as the gilt-framed antique oil painting, carved bed, and nubby natural floor covering—freshen the room with contemporary country flair.

in the pink in any room

WD239
Ultra Blue

WP237

WP242
Blue Blossom

WP248
Summer Blue

WP249
Sky Blue

WT254
Dover Blue

at home with SKY

"Blue color is everlastingly appointed

sky

Is there any pleasure more simple and profound than lying in the grass under the Earth's clear blue canopy and watching a parade of wispy white clouds float by? In fact, Mother Nature has created an abundance of blue and white bliss: morning glories clinging to a white trellis; blueberries and cream; hydrangeas in a milk-glass pitcher; the eyes of a trusted friend. Not surprisingly, blue and white is one of the most enduring palettes. Weavers, painters, and potters have all taken cues from this natural pairing, creating the gingham, denim, willowware, flow-blue, delft tiles, and the blue and cream of Wedgwood jasperware that we use to decorate our homes. Blue symbolizes constancy and truth, hope and faithfulness, sincerity and endurance. "If you love me (but not quite) / Send me a ribbon, a ribbon of white," goes a child's rhyme. "If you love me, love me true / Send me a ribbon, a ribbon of blue." If you are loyal, you are "true-blue." After all, no matter how many gray, stormy days there are, the

y the Deity to be a source of delight."

— JOHN RUSKIN, *Lectures on Architecture and Painting*

blue sky will always return. Blue and white can be crisp and clean or dreamy and serene. Pale blue gives a room the sense of infinite space; dark blue makes a room feel enclosed and safe. No matter the exact shade, reflecting on the color of the sky seems to have a restorative effect. It lowers blood pressure, respiration, and heart rate. The brain's response is one of relax-

ation. "We love to contemplate blue, not because it advances to us," wrote Goethe in *Theory of Colors*, "but because it draws us after it."

sky

Just as blue and white can be a navy suit with a starched white shirt or blue jeans and a white T-shirt, it can be formal or casual in your home too. The fusion of casual and formal elements that is the hallmark of the Town & Country style helps ease the visual transition between this living room and breakfast room. The Navajo-inspired print on the sofa is casual; the motif on the pillow and valances—a bird of paradise—is more formal. The white painted chairs are cottage-style casual; the crisp pleated slipcovers are more formal, but in a breezy, country-style plaid. A classic and versatile blue and white color scheme ties the contrasting styles together.

same colors
different styles
TOWN & COUNTRY

The graciousness of European living is evident in this pretty and fresh living room. Inspired by French and English classics, it is not the least bit stuffy, thanks to the creative use of color and scale. The color scheme revolves around primaries that are muted enough to be sophisticated. English willowware and blue and white floral fabric give the room its main color theme. Provençal yellow on the walls adds sunny warmth; so do the draperies with their accents of ocher and red. The paisley print on the ottoman is a traditional motif, but it's done in an airy and lighthearted oversize scale.

BEAUTIFUL THINGS

sky

If you love the classic and crisp look of blue and white but yearn for a little spot of warmth and brightness, look upward. After all, the big yellow sun looks just right amid all of that blue and white. Yellow is a lovely counterpoint to the sky palette. In blue's primary color family, red adds heat, but yellow provides a softer, sunshiny warmth to a room. It doesn't take much yellow to visually "pop" in a mostly blue and white room. In this casual living room, there's just a hint of it in the upholstered ottoman and wing chair. Both pieces are predominantly blue, but the yellow brings a pleasant brightness to the blue and white scheme. The yellow accent is underscored by accessories: a soft fleece throw and a teapot full of fresh flowers. A creamy white rug and a few pieces of painted white furniture keep the room firmly rooted in the freshness of blue and white. If you would like a few more rays of yellow, add them in a subtle pattern in the draperies or in a few more accessories, such as throw pillows or Provençal-style yellow-glazed pottery.

bring a spot of sunshine inside

sky

looking for **accents** in
all the right places

Even in a nearly monochromatic scheme, as in this bold sapphire-blue foyer, an accent color in small doses will bring the scheme to life. A room's accent might come from a yellow pine floor, cherry woodwork, or a mahogany dining room set. You can build the room around such features or furnishings, or you can choose a color scheme that will benefit from these preexisting accents. Here, the wicker chairs and a light wood table and mirror frame introduce a pale yellow into the blue space; the warm notes are highlighted with straw yellow in the upholstery, the screen and cushion fabric, and the Picassoesque painting. These touches provide visual relief without diluting the drama.

sky

A blue and white kitchen is a classic for a good reason: The kitchen is prone to the clutter of cookware, dishes, and food items, but the crisp, clean combination of blue and white keeps the room looking fresh and tidy. This mostly white kitchen gets an accent from the blue ceramice tile backsplash. Bursts of color and a mix of blue and white patterns keep it from looking sterile. Country-style gingham curtains soften the walls, and striped cushions with coordinating floral ties literally soften the seats of the Prussian blue chairs. A toile tablecloth adds a touch of sophisticated pattern. Combining it with checks and stripes creates visual interest and a casual feeling; you could use toile throughout for a dressier effect.

blue and white is crisp and clean

left Any culinary purist will tell you that white dishes are the best choice for showing off the exquisite colors and shapes of foods. They are also versatile. Choose white dishes for flexibility, then enhance your table setting with colorful accessories, such as cobalt blue bowls and glassware. With basic white dishware, what is underneath the dishes—in this case, a classic blue and white toile tablecloth topped with subtle blue plaid napkins—can be changed to reflect the season, the occasion, or even your mood.

left When you have glass-door cabinets, you accomplish two homemaking feats at once—you store and decorate at the same time. Choose dishes and glassware in a saturated color or in simple shapes and patterns and then arrange them on the shelves. Your tableware will be neatly tucked away, and it will create a burst of color in what would otherwise be a blank spot—or one muddled with pieces of disparate colors.

Get toned up (and down)

The adage, "Blue and green should never be seen" is sorely misleading. Nearly any two colors can be used together in the same room as long as they are similar in tone. Tone refers to how light or dark a color is. Different intensities of different colors can create visual dissonance. Blue and green are beautiful together—and so are blue and white—when the intensity of each color is in the same range. In the bedroom, *top right*, the blue is a soft, powdery blue, and the white is a decidedly creamy yellow-white. The art on the wall, *right*, has vivid blues, oranges, and yellows (and a brilliant white mat) whose tones are compatible with the sapphire-blue wall.

sky

soft colors, suite dreams

A soft pillow and a firm mattress might give the sheep an assist in getting you to sleep at night, but a scheme of dreamy colors can be almost as effective. Research has shown that blue has a soothing effect on the body. This powdery wedgwood blue, together with a soft, creamy white, whispers repose. The print in the bedding is small and quiet, rather than large and bold. When creating a somnolent hideaway, consider adding relaxation-inducing accessories: a fleece or soft wool throw to snuggle under while you read; lots of pillows to lounge on; and even a gauzy canopy if your bed frame allows. A pretty carafe and drinking glass for water by the bedside are a nice touch too.

The classic, highly versatile combination of blue and white is found the world over, from cottages to castles. It can be formal, casual, or somewhere in between, depending on the tones of the colors, the ratio of blue to white, and its expression in pattern. In this dining room, *left*, a large floral print on the draperies and slipcovers, stately striped wallpaper, and all-white furniture lend a comfortable formality to the room. With its bright blue

blue and white, always right

color and fun animal-print wallpaper border and bedding, this little boy's room, *above*, is ready for snails, puppy-dog tails, and lots of activity. In the dining room, *right*, soft, ruffle-topped floral-print draperies, a distressed-pine buffet, a glass-top dining table, and Swedish-style chairs create an atmosphere that is formal enough for special occasions but casual enough for weeknight meals.

sky

the many moods of blue

Blue and white isn't just one color scheme. It takes in a multitude of shades, tints, and accent colors that make the possibilities for beautiful blue and white rooms as limitless as the sky that inspired the scheme. Both of these bathrooms are blue and white; both have stripes. But the rooms look entirely different, starting with the tones of blue and white. The bathroom, *opposite*, is done in shades of navy and a creamy, almost muslin white. The prevailing accent color is decidedly neutral. The result is a cottage-by-the-seaside feel, as though the room looked right out onto the Cape. In the bathroom, *right*, a brighter blue and the strong presence of yellow sets a different mood. It's cheery and whimsical, an aquatic playground for little ones where rubber ducky and his crew are right at home.

at home with SPICE

spice

Imagine an open-air market in a city in Morocco or India. Its stalls overflow with baskets of spices that entice with their aromas, flavors, and colors: paprika, nutmeg, saffron, cumin, chilies, mustard, ginger, cinnamon, cloves, allspice. The heat of the sun creates the heat and color of spices, so it is no surprise that the spice palette is suffused with warmth and sensuality. The embracing tones of this palette take wing from the sun-warmed terra-cotta tiles of an Italian piazza, a field of mustard flowers in Provence, the saffron-colored robes of Buddhist monks, and a bowl of oranges in a warm kitchen. Spice colors are as versatile as they are easy to live with. They add depth to small spaces and make large spaces warm and welcoming. They are earthy and strong without being overpowering. Spice colors have energy without being frenetic. They are nurturing, comfortable, contented, and protective. The art of Vincent van Gogh reflects his love for this palette, particularly the deep yellow tones of mustard, ocher, and saffron, which he felt were "capable of charming God." Spice tones are naturally present in the material that has most commonly given humans shelter: wood. From the warm yellows of country pine to the rich reddish-brown of highly polished mahogany, wood tones exemplify and embody this palette. Spice colors also reflect the deep, embracing comforts of home: the burnished orange of well-used copper pots; the golden-brown crust of a freshly baked loaf of bread or crisp-roasted chicken; a cup of hot coffee or tea; and the mottled browns of a woodpile stocked to fuel cozy fires.

spice

same colors different styles
COLORS OF PROVENCE

E ven if you live miles from Marseilles, your home can take on a distinctively French accent with the help of vibrant Provençal color. One of the most ubiquitous hues in the Provençal palette is saffron. Here, the largest piece of furniture, the sofa, is covered in a monochromatic yellow stripe that looks nearly solid. As a result, despite the different prints in the chair, valances, rug, and pillows, the room looks airy and clean. The prints work well together because of their limited palette—mostly saffron and red—and similar scale. The undulating valances add interest to the windows without overwhelming the room, while sheers let in lots of that fabled Provençal sunlight.

spice

same colors different styles

TOWN & COUNTRY

The balance of artfulness and comfort that is Town & Country can be achieved with rich colors from the more muted side of the spice palette—those that look pleasingly timeworn. Toile, a classic, elegant print, conveys a casual yet sophisticated style; the fabric's dusty persimmon color, *above* and *opposite*, is soft, subtle, and inviting. The profusion of pillows on the sofa begs you to plop down; those framed in a muted, nutmeg-brown fabric ask you to contemplate the beauty of their art. The bold stripes of the chair fabric lend an architectural element to the room, while the pumpkin-hued throws tossed over them add comfort. Small touches, such as the art book and the bouquet of dried berries, *right*, demonstrate that art and nature intertwine beautifully.

spice

spice colors
work throughout
the seasons

I f the rich fall colors of the
spice palette have drawn
you in, you need not worry
that your home will be
suspended in an eternal autumn.
You can live comfortably year-
round with this palette if you
strike a balance of color. In this
living room, white and light
colors in the "envelope" of the
room (the walls, ceiling, and
floor) keep the upholstered
pieces from looking too heavy.
In fact, the largest piece, the sofa,
is also covered in an all-season
creamy white fabric. Take
texture into account, too, when
aiming for a seasonless spice
look. Here, the rustic weave of
wicker in a tray and basket
lightens the mood of the room
and softens the formality of the
naturally rich spice palette.

Autumnal tones can feel light and airy with the right balance of color and

an array of objects, textures, and elements that change the mood.

opposite The principle of balance is one of the keys to a successfully decorated room. The tones of all the colors in this room are similar; even the deep, creamy white of the sofa is in keeping with the rich shades of orange and rust. All of the colors have a similar balance of lightness and darkness. Balance is central to good design not only when you are choosing colors; balanced patterns are just as important as balanced colors. Despite their different patterns, the throw pillows work well together because the paisley and floral print are similar in scale. With a solid-color pillow in the middle, each pattern remains distinct and fresh to the eye.

above Accessories and accents in colors from the lighter side of the spice family— such as the mustard-yellow bowl, the deep tangerine of the throw, and the bouquet of orange-tipped roses—prevent a naturally enveloping palette from becoming overbearing. If you want to lighten up even more during the spring and summer months, consider slipcovering chairs and pillows in colors from the softer end of the spice spectrum: tones of tan, ocher, or persimmon.

spice

set a welcoming tone

Nothing says "welcome" more eloquently than an entryway that is awash in a rich, warm, embracing color, such as the toasty terra-cotta that covers this foyer. The warmth of the color sets the mood, but the furnishings and accessories offer true hospitality. A broad cushion-covered bench outfitted with soft pillows in pretty prints invites guests (and your family) to sit down and take off shoes and coats comfortably. A hall tree for hanging up coats quickly and a handsomely framed mirror for last-minute inspections might be other niceties to consider placing in an entryway.

left Solid-color walls call for something to break up the monotony. Here, that notion was taken a step further, in draperies sewn of two different patterns from the same spice color family. To keep the space airy and inviting, the smaller print was used on top and for most of the length, with a broad band of a splashy floral on the bottom. The transition between the two prints is softened by a ribbon of fringe that is both whimsical and functional.

Many of today's new homes are being built with grandiose entryways and very high ceilings throughout. If you play professional basketball and appreciate the headroom, these features may feel wonderful; but if you feel a little bereft in such a place, you can make it feel more intimate by your color and pattern choices. The colors of the spice palette can warm a "tall" room. The mustard-hued walls in the kitchen, *opposite*, and the paprika-colored walls in the living room, *left*, advance, making the rooms seem smaller to the viewer. The pattern of the wallpaper also advances the walls. Most importantly, though, wallpaper borders in both rooms visually lower the ceiling, beautifying and defining the space where the wall meets the ceiling.

short on comfort?
cozy up a tall room

WP143
Zanzari White

WP136
Snow White

WP291
Shadow Green

WP299
Crystal

at home with WHITES

"White is the most vital thing in nature; it

whites

The deliciousness of decorating with white lies in its simplicity, its timeless perfection, and its tremendous breadth of tones. White is not one color, but many colors. In the language of the Inuit, the indigenous people of Alaska, there are more than a hundred words for describing the painterly gradations of white in the arctic landscape. The luminescence of white appears in eggshells, pearls, lilies, and sweet-smelling gardenias. There is the creamy white of raw cotton, the blue-white of marble, the yellow-white interior of a slice of ripe pear. In our homes, white is the color of painted wicker, lace curtains, matelassé coverlets, and goose-down

reverberates from silk differently from snow."

——WALTER SARGEANT, *The Enjoyment and Use of Color*

pillows. White is the color of purity, peace, and tranquillity. White is nostalgic: There is an innocence to white; it is the color of youth—of christening dresses and wedding gowns—and of simple pleasures: a game of tennis or a round of croquet in crisp white apparel on a summer afternoon, an ice cream social on the lawn of a white clapboard country church. White can be spare and minimalist, too, as in the

Moderne style of the 1930s, which popularized textured off-white wallpaper and creamy white upholstery. Even in minimalist style, however, white is still subtle and soft—a sigh rather than a shout. "The red rose whispers of passion / And the white rose breathes of love," wrote poet John Boyle O'Reilly in *A White Rose*. "O, the red rose is a falcon / And the white rose is a dove."

same colors
different styles

BEAUTIFUL THINGS

I f you are of the mind that heaven can't wait, create your own slice of paradise with the color scheme that surely makes the angels sing: white and metallic gold. The 18th-century English-style mahogany dining table with brass-footed legs, *opposite*, sets the traditional tone in this Beautiful Things dining room—but an abundance of airy white keeps the room from being stuffy. Although the space is mostly white, romantic gilt accents on the valance, *opposite*, and on the mirror frame, tableware, and gold-braid trim on the napkins, *above* and *right*, give shape to the room and keep it from looking washed-out. Crisp pleated slipcovers with ties, *opposite*, impart a softness to the space and can be removed in a snap for easy cleaning.

same colors
different styles
PAST PERFECT

Creamy white, the color of old-fashioned vanilla ice cream, is the key to creating the nostalgic Past Perfect look. The yellow-toned white used in this rustic dining area has the pleasingly timeworn look of vintage hand-stitched linens. Against the dark, rough-hewn plank walls, the textured tablecloth and gauzy, white-on-white slipcovers create a fresh, sophisticated interpretation of country style. The sheerness of the fabric offsets the warm tones of the wood and holds its own in this setting because it trades volume for weight. The billowy, gathered skirts reach to the floor; the opaque fabric still lets light through. The effect is breezy and supremely comfortable—like a summer dress on a warm day.

Which white is white?

Is white really a color? In pigment or dye form, it is technically achromatic, which means "without color." But in terms of light, white contains all of the colors of the spectrum: red, orange, yellow, green, blue, indigo, and violet. Consequently, there are hundreds of whites. The human eye perceives pure white—one without a hint of another color— as brilliant and glaring. The whites we use to decorate our homes are tinted with just a touch of a color: with yellow to create a creamy white; with blue, black (which creates a gray-white), pink, or green. That is why some whites seem cool and others seem warm. Texture comes into play too. A nubby fabric reflects less light than a shiny porcelain plate. Even if they are the same tone of white, the fabric will appear to be a dull white; the plate, a brighter white.

Just as white itself relies on a whisper of pure color to give it some life, an all-white decorating scheme needs a little something to stand out from its canvas and attract the eye. Any color may be used as an accent in a white room; look for clues in your furnishings, tapestries, pieces of art, or collectibles. Here, the corkscrew black legs of the modern-style chairs are paired with a pattern of almost black navy and white. Blue and gray are closely related, so the pearl gray pillows on the sofa work with the blue and white fabric. After all, gray is simply white tinted with black (and sometimes tones of other colors, too, such as blue). The warm quality of the gray and the ruffled trim on the pillows lend softness to a space that could otherwise appear stark. When it comes to mixing whites, be fearless: Note that here, creamy-white throw pillows comfortably flank a crisp, bright white one.

add a little accent
to an all-white room

make white on white warm and welcoming

Do you have a zest for life? Consider creating a kitchen that is both functional and fun, using an overall white scheme bursting with fresh citrus tones. A white kitchen is an easy choice because it always looks fresh and clean, but it can be stark if it lacks all color. To prevent that, a creamy, yellow-toned white was applied to the walls and cabinets here. Extrapolating from that warm tone, the Klimt-inspired painting infuses the room with shades of lemon and lime. The table settings—linens and dishes—can incorporate the creamy white as well as the citrus tones. For a fun and fitting centerpiece, consider a pyramid of lemons or limes in a pretty white compote.

warm up white with neutrals

The snowy winter landscape provides ample encouragement for warming up an all-white color scheme with the neutral colors of autumn leaves and moss-covered bark. In this tranquil guest bedroom, the fabric panels behind the bed, the pillows, and the curtain feature white fabric with a neutral accent, or vice versa. The fabric panels warm up the room with color and act as backdrops for the headboards, adding softness and dimension to the all-white walls. When working with different whites in adjoining rooms, you can use one tone of white as the main color in the first room, applying accents of the other white; then reverse the scheme in the next room. Or apply two or three shades of white in equal amounts in both rooms.

pattern comes into play

When a room is wrapped all (or mostly) in white, texture and pattern become especially important in establishing the look and feel of the space. The pattern can be white on white—either in a texture or in shades of white—or it can appear in an accent color. In the dining room, *opposite*, pattern appears in the sculpted square-medallion texture of the creamy white tablecloth; the toile wallpaper and striped slipcovers employ black—the yin to white's yang—to create another pleasing pattern. In the living room, *left,* wallpaper with a hint of cornflower blue freshens the mostly white room. The decorative mirror echoes the floral pattern in the wallpaper. To create an interesting white decorating scheme, build on the patterns and motifs in your favorite accessories, such as antique china, a piece of needlework, or a matelassé coverlet.

resources

See something you love? Here's where to go for more information.

Note: Fabrics, paints, wallpapers and accessories shown in this book were available from Waverly as of the date of publication. Items may be discontinued without notice; if a fabric or wallpaper you like is no longer available, call consumer information at 800/423-5881 for help in finding a substitute. For more information on Waverly fabrics, wallpapers, ready-made bed linens and accessories, or made-to-order window and bed treatments, visit the website at www.waverly.com or call 800/423-5881. For more information on Waverly paint, call 800/631-3440.

PAGE 4: Chair cushions front: Botanica 665391, Chair cushions side and back: Bedford Cord 647891 Pillow: Ranger 609848

PAGE 6: Chair: McCheck 608021

PAGE 8: Neutrals: Fabrics: Congo 665290; Homespun Check 647952; Homespun Gingham 647962; Nicole 647355; Waverly paint chips (Norton & Son); Wallpaper: Natural Weaves 574670; Crimson: Fabrics: Heritage 647064; Essex Ivy 665673; Cumbria 665712; Newton 665625; Le Soleil 647461; Heritage 647066; Jewel: Fabrics: Caribe 609877; Ottoman 647018; Brookfield Check 647407; Windsor Washed Velvet 631565; Limerick 647117; Waverly paint chips (Norton & Son)

PAGE 9: Spring: Fabrics: Party Plaid 647303; Party Plaid 647302; Perfection 647203; Bedford Cord 647658; Dennisport 647870; Oakbluff 647913; Tulip Trance 665922; Waverly paint chips (Norton & Son); Sky: Wallpaper: Waterman Stripe 5722595; Waverly paint chips (Norton & Son); Fabrics: Country Life Toile 659431; Nichole 647354 (napkin); Nicoletta 647444; Spice: Fabrics: Fredrik 663991; Wellington 665022; Windsor Washed Velvet 631562; Heritage 647066; Watermark 647635; Paint chips: Waverly (Norton & Son); Whites: Waverly paint chips (Norton & Son); Fabrics: Duette White 614810; Le Soleil 647460; Perfection 647190; Zig Zag 647610; Capulet 647320; Bedford Cord 647650

PAGE 12: Waverly Loose Back Sofa (Lexington) covered in Minicheck 647500; Pillow: Chantal 665771

PAGE 13: Waverly lamp (Robert Abbey); Lampshade: Pimlico Plaid 647794; Top pillow: Kensington 647805; Bottom pillow: Shawl Stripe: 647782

PAGE 14: Chair: Le Soleil 647462

PAGE 15: Waverly paint (Norton & Son): Barn WA189; Chair slipcovers: Oriental Toile 665371; Napkins: Watermark Ruby 647636; Top tablecloth: Homespun Gingham 647961; Under tablecloth: 632431

PAGE 16: Sofa: Bedouin Stripe 664700; Pillows: Sasha 664720

PAGE 17: Screen and pillows: Zig Zag 647615; Zig Zag 647614; Limerick 647117; Limerick 647008; Bedford Cord 647657

PAGE 19: Sofa: Silk Strie 664617; Pillows: Heritage 647063; Curtains: Pimlico Plaid 647794; Ottoman: Cumbria 665710; Waverly rug (Beaulieu): Chelsea WA102

PAGE 20: Chair: Zig Zag 647611

PAGE 21: Chair cushion and pillow: Cumbria Red 665712; Curtains: Newton 665625; Chair: Essex Ivy 665673

PAGE 22: Table runner: Silk Strie 664619; Tablecloth: Vintage Floral 665470; Seat cushion front: Vintage Floral 665470; Seat cushion back: Silk Strie 664619; Waverly rug 5094F-2 Roseberry

PAGE 23: Sofa: Wellington 665022; Ottoman: Windsor Washed Velvet 631562; Chair: Stockholm Stripe 647263

PAGE 24: Neutrals: Chairs: Tahiti 665210; Tablecloth: Gulf Stream 665280; Crimson: Waverly dining table 565-873; Waverly dining chairs 565883 upholstered in Kensington 647804; Waverly rug (Feizy): Roseberry 5094F-Z; Curtains: Dorset 66563; Place mats: Perfection 647204, Fulham 665641; Napkins: Buckingham 665721; Waverly paint (Norton & Son): Cardinal WA187

PAGE 25: Waverly furniture (Lexington): Loose Back Sofa in Minicheck 647500; Tight Back Chair 7948-11 and Semi-attached Top Ottoman 7948-44 in Chantal 665771; Side chairs: Checkpoint 647750; Waverly Rug (Feizy): Rochelle 4267F2 Gold/Red; Pillows: Dominique 665562; Curtain (sheer): Miller 614830

PAGE 26: Neutrals: Pillows: Brookfield Check 647401, Dragonflies Needlepoint L1447CHM, Brookfield 647411; Crimson: Waverly furniture (Lexington): Dining table 565-873; Huntboard 565-862; Dining chairs 01-0565-880; Waverly paint (Norton & Son): Cardinal WA187; Seat cushions (back): Pimlico Plaid 64779; Seat cushions (front): Kensington Coral 647804; Place mats: Perfection 647204, Fulham 665641; Napkins: Buckingham 665721; Jewel: Headboard: Ceasar 647513

PAGE 27: Spring: Napkin: Buckingham 665721; Place mat: Season's Texture 647480; Waverly

glasses (Zrieke): Bijoux; Waverly salad plate (Zrieke): Gazebo; Dining chair covered in Nicole 647353; Waverly rug (Feizy): Yellow Gazebo 4228F-3; Sky: Waverly lamp (Robert Abbey); Lampshade: Pimlico Plaid 647794; Bottom pillow: Shawl Stripe 647782; Top pillow: Kensington 647805; Spice: Chair: Monroe Paisley 665311; Pillow: Heritage 64706; Whites: Sofa: Heritage 647050; Pillows: Zig Zag 647611, Zig Zag 647610, Old World Linen 645618

PAGES 28-29: Fabrics: Congo 665290; Homespun Check 647952; Homespun Gingham 647962; Nicole 647355; Waverly paint chips (Norton & Son); Wallpaper: Natural Weaves 574670

PAGES 32-33: Roman shade: Zig Zag 647611; Drapes: Silk Tweed 632431; Slipcovers: Tahiti 665210; Tablecloth: Gulf Stream 665280

PAGE 34: Slipcovers: Tahiti 665210 Tablecloth: Gulf Stream 665280

PAGE 35: Napkins: Tahiti 665210

PAGE 36: Napkins: Tahiti 665210

PAGE 37: Slipcovers and pillow: Tahiti 665210; Tablecloth: Gulf Stream 665280; Waverly rug (Feizy): Green Tribal Tapestry 8154F

PAGE 38: Roman Shade: Homespun Check 647952; Tablecloth: Homespun Check 647952; Underskirt: Homespun Solid 647982; Chair cushions: Homespun Gingham 647962

PAGE 39: Tablecloth: Homespun Check 647952

PAGES 40-41: Curtains: Brookfield 647411; Sofa slipcovers: Old World Linen 645603; Pillows: Brookfield Check 64740, Tiger Needlepoint L1446CHM

PAGE 42: Sofa: Old World Linen 645603; Pillows: Brookfield Check 647401; Pillow: Tiger Needlepoint L1446CHM

PAGE 43: Pillows: Brookfield Check 647401, Dragonflies Needlepoint L1447CHM, Brookfield 647411

PAGES 44-45: Comforter top: Autumn Leaves 665090; Comforter back: Seasonings 665140; Curtain and valance: Garden Patch 665120; Pillows: Seasons Plaid 647472, Pressed Leaves 665100; Bed skirt: Seasonings 665140; Chair: Seasons Texture 647482; Curtain on door: Pressed Leaves 665100; Waverly paint (Norton & Son): Colonial Khaki WT153; Tawny WT132; Classic Cream WT130

PAGES 46-47: Shower curtain: Check Mate 664211

PAGE 48: Wallpaper: Tahiti 577700; Roman shade: Gulf Stream: 665280

PAGE 49: Wallpaper (above chair rail): Ashland Leaf 579385; Wallpaper border: Topiary Studies 578830; Wallpaper (below chair rail): Ashby 579370

PAGE 50: Wallpaper: Mandan Scroll 579253; Mandan 579233; Border: Blackwell 574533; Sofa: Tapestry 646061

PAGE 51: Wallpaper: Paradise Island Companion: 577751, Havana 577805; Shower curtain: Gulf Stream: 665281

PAGES 52-53: Fabrics: Heritage 647064; Essex Ivy 665673; Cumbria 665712; Newton 665625; Le Soleil 647461; Heritage 647066

PAGE 55: Wall fabric: Mayenne 665700; Chairs: Le Soleil 647461; Waverly paint (Norton & Son): Cinnabar WA188

PAGE 56: Chair slipcovers: Oriental Toile 665371; Top tablecloth: Homespun Gingham 647961; Under tablecloth: 645603; Waverly glassware: Veranda Clear 3202370; Pillows: Tidewater 665331; Providence Check 647562; Bench seat cushion: Homespun Gingham 647961

PAGE 57: Chair slipcovers: Oriental Toile 665371; Top tablecloth:

Homespun Gingham 647961; Under tablecloth: 645603; Waverly glassware: Veranda Clear 3202370; Waverly paint (Norton & Son): Barn WA189; Napkins: Watermark Ruby 647636; Bench seat cushion: Homespun Gingham 647961; Pillows: Tidewater 665331

PAGE 58: Waverly paint (Norton & Son): Cardinal WA187; Waverly rug (Feizy): Roseberry 5094F-Z; Waverly chairs (Lexington); Upholstered armchair: 565883

PAGE 59: Waverly dining table 565-873; Waverly rug (Feizy): 5094F-Z; Curtains: Dorset 66563; Seat cushions (front): Kensington 647804; Place mats: Perfection 647204, Fulham 665641; Napkins: Buckingham 665721

PAGE 60: Waverly paint (Norton & Son): Cardinal WA187; Curtains: Dorset 665641; Waverly chairs (Lexington); Seat cushions (front) Kensington 647804; Seat cushions (back): Pimlico Plaid 64779

PAGE 61: Waverly furniture (Lexington): Dining table 565-873; Huntboard 565-862; Arm chair 01-0565-881; Side chair 01-0565-880; Waverly paint (Norton & Son): Cardinal WA187; Seat cushions (back): Pimlico Plaid 64779; Place mats: Perfection 647204, Fulham 665641; Napkins: Buckingham 665721

PAGES 62-63: Pillows: Essex Ivy 665673, Cumbria Red 665712; Sofa: Le Soleil 647461; Curtains: Newton 665625

PAGE 64: Curtains: Newton 665625; Sofa: Le Soleil 647461; Pillows: Newton 665625, Essex Ivy 665673; Chair: Essex Ivy 665673

PAGE 65: Cushion: Cumbria Red 665712; Pillows: Essex Ivy 665673; Le Soleil 647461, Newton 665625

PAGE 66: Curtains: Pimlico Plaid 647791; Pillow: Georgian Rose 665660; Seat cushion: Shawl Stripe 647780

PAGE 67: Comforter front: Georgian Rose 665660; Bed skirt, comforter back: Pimlico Plaid 647791; Eurosham: Heirloom Ticking 662750; Coverlet: Le Soleil 647465

PAGES 68-69: Wall fabric: Mayenne 665700; Chairs: Le Soleil 647461; Waverly paint (Norton & Son): Cinnabar WA188

PAGE 70: Wallpaper: Avignon Stripe

5500320; Wallpaper border: Avignon 5500310; Chair: Calais 664620

PAGE 71: Wallpaper: Mistral Cloud 575870; Wallpaper border: Rochelle 5500250; Tablecloth, valance: Lyon 664660

PAGES 72-73: Fabrics: Caribe 609877; Ottoman 647018; Brookfield Check 647407; Windsor Washed Velvet 631565; Limerick 647117; Waverly paint chips (Norton & Son)

PAGE 75: Place mat: Zig Zag 647616/Mitered in Zig Zag 647617; Napkins: Bedouin Stripe 664700

PAGES 76-77: Screen and pillows: Zig Zag 647615; Zig Zag 647614; Limerick 647116; Limerick 647117; Limerick 647008; Bedford Cord 647657

PAGE 79: Pillows: Zig Zag 647615; Zig Zag 647614; Limerick 647116; Limerick 647117; Limerick 647008; Bedford Cord 647657

PAGES 80-81: Floor pillow: Caribe 609877; Sofa: Town & Country Velvet 602782; Pillows: Botanica 665391, Ranger 609848, Caribe 609877

PAGE 82: Curtains and pillow: Botanica 665391; Chair: Caribe 609877

PAGE 83: Pillows: Botanica 665391, Ranger 609848, Caribe 609877; Ottoman: 647016

PAGE 84: Napkins: Bedouin Stripe 664700; Place mats: Zig Zag 647616/Mitered in Zig Zag 647617; Seat cushions: Sasha 664720

PAGE 85: Sofa: Bedouin Stripe 664700; Pillows: Sasha 664720; Napkins: Bedouin Stripe 664700; Place mats: Zig Zag 647616/Mitered in Zig Zag 647617

PAGE 86: Headboard: Ceasar 647513; Curtains: Windsor Washed Velvet 631565; Headboard: Caesar 647513; Comforter front: Brookfield Check 647407; Comforter back and pillow sham: Caesar 647514

PAGE 88: Curtains: Windsor Washed Velvet 631565; Comforter front: Brookfield Check 647407; Comforter back and pillow sham: Caesar 647514

PAGE 89: Headboard: Caesar 647513; Comforter back and pillow sham: Caesar 647514

PAGE 90: Wallpaper: Bremen Companion 572961, Tapestry-Salzburg Companion 572991; Border: Bremen 572971; Chairs: Bremen 663911; Window treatment: Windsor

Washed Velvet 631561

PAGE 91: Border: Castille 572922; Wallpaper: Aragon 572932; Ceiling: Salerno 573178; Pillows: Aragon 663742, Luxurious 630423; Curtains: Greenbriar Damask 631551

PAGES 92-93: Fabrics: Party Plaid 647303; Party Plaid 647302; Perfection 647203; Bedford Cord 647658; Dennisport 647870; Oakbluff 647913; Tulip Trance 665922; Waverly paint chips (Norton & Sons)

PAGE 96: Waverly Tight Back Chaise: (Lexington) 7824-75 covered in Heritage 647063; Curtains: Pimlico Plaid 647794; Ottoman and pillow: Cumbria 665710

PAGE 97: Sofa: Silk Strie 664617; Curtains: Pimlico Plaid 647794; Ottoman, pillow, and table skirt: Cumbria 665710; Lampshade: Fulham 665642; Waverly rug (Beaulieu): Chelsea WA102

PAGE 98: Chair back: Dennisport 647708; Chair front: Vineyard Ticking 647688; Pillows: Dennisport 647871, Northampton 665730

PAGE 99: Sofa: Vineyard Ticking 647688; Chair back: Dennisport 647708; Chair front: Vineyard Ticking: 647688; Pillows: Dennisport 647871, Northampton 665730; Waverly rug (Beaulieu): Papyrus 4536

PAGE 100: Waverly rug (Feizy): Yellow Gazebo 4228F-3; Waverly furniture (Lexington): Side chair 563884 covered in Nicole 647353; Rectangular Dining Table 563-877; Le Fleur Door Chest 566-972

PAGE 102: Waverly furniture (Lexington): Le Fleur Door Chest 566-972; Curtains: Pimlico Plaid 647794; Waverly glassware (Zrieke): Gazebo pitcher 9755240; Bijoux Green glasses 3200290

PAGE 103: Napkin: Buckingham 665721; Place mat: Seasons Texture 647480; Waverly glasses (Zrieke): Bijoux 3200270; Waverly salad plate (Zrieke): Gazebo 000000

PAGE 104: Chair: Le Soleil 647462

PAGE 105: Chair: Le Soleil 647462; Comforter front: Dorset 665632; Comforter back: Fulham 665642; Euroshams: Le Soleil 647468; Pillows: Sussex 665651

PAGES 106-107: Shower curtain: Paradise Island 665222; Waverly paint

resources

(Norton & Son): Mint Ice WP293
PAGE 108: Wallpaper (top): Vienne 575691; Wallpaper (bottom): Mini Gingham 575761; Border: Josette 575811; Pillows: Vienne 664651; Bedspread and neckroll: Le Soleil 647461

PAGE 109: Border: Meadow Way 575382; Comforter front and ruffled pillow: Meadow Way 664582; Wallpaper: Portland Stripe 5750892; Valance: Nichole Check 647363; Pillow with ties: Nichole Check 647363 (body), Nicole (ties) 647353; Eurosham: Nicole Check 647363, Nicole 647353 (flange); Comforter back: Nicole Check 647363, Nicole 647353; Table skirt: Meadow Way 664582; Border: Nicole 647353; Ivory sheer: AB441441084; Under sheer: Nicole 647353

PAGE 110: Wallpaper: Heirloom Poppy Toss 5500054, Heirloom Leaf 5500064, Heirloom Poppies 5500044; Wallpaper border: Heirloom Poppy 5500034; Slipcovers: Tiny Check 647662

PAGE 111: Wallpaper border: Bruton Bouquet 576761; Wallpaper: Bruton Vine 576771; Comforter and pillow sham: Bruton Bouquet 665341; Duvet and Eurosham: Lafayette Plaid 647591

PAGES 112-113: Wallpaper: Waterman Stripe 5722595; Waverly paint chips (Norton & Son); Fabrics: Country Life Toile 659431; Nichole 647354 (napkin); Nicoletta 647444

PAGE 116: Sofa and inside liner of valance: Tuckahoe 665350; Window valance and pillow: Tidewater Resist 665330; Chair skirts: Providence Check 647563

PAGE 117: Drapes: Rochelle 664683; Drapery lining: Lyon 664662; Seat cushions: Vienne 664652; Upholstered chair: La Petite Ferme 664674; Ottoman: Alsace 664642; Blanket/throw: Toulouse 664692; Loveseat: Heritage 647051/Piped in Petite Paisley 647492; Pillows: Calais 664622, Vienne 664652, Toulouse 664692

PAGES 118-119: Sofa: Veranda Stripe 648243; Ottoman: Cortona 648255; Wing chair: Margrette 648202; Pillow:

Capulet Stripe 666653; Curtains: Market Square Sheer 615443

PAGES 120-121: Chair cushions: Wellesley 647271; Pillows: Newport 647291; Waverly paint (Norton & Son): Flag Blue WA245; Screen: Greenwich 647281

PAGES 122-123: Tablecloth: Country Life Toile 659431/Mitered in Cadet Blue 647019; Napkin: Nichole 647354; Seat cushions: Wellesley 647271

PAGE 124: Tablecloth: Country Life Toile 659431/Mitered in Cadet Blue 647019; Napkin: Nichole 647354

PAGE 125: Waverly glassware (Zrieke): Veranda Blue 3202170, Veranda Blue 3202190 (12-ounce), Bijou 3200170 (8-ounce); Top pillow: Kensington 647805; Bottom pillow: Shawl Stripe 647782; Waverly lamp (Robert Abbey); Lampshade: Pimlico Plaid 647794

PAGES 126-127: Top pillow: Kensington 647805; Coverlet front, bottom pillow: Shawl Stripe 647782; Coverlet back: Limerick 647115; Waverly lamp (Robert Abbey); Lampshade: Pimlico Plaid 647794

PAGE 128: Dining Room: Wallpaper border: Garden Toile 575833; Wallpaper: Garden Toile Stripe 57863, Garden Toile: 575453; Slipcovers: Garden Toile 664573; Child's Room: Wallpaper border: Animal Walk 574352; Wallpaper: Arbor Strie 573387, Leopard Skin 574372; Duvet and window treatment: Animal Kingdom 66422; Bean bag: Check Mate 664214

PAGE 129: Wallpaper border: Regent Bamboo 578633; Wallpaper: Knightsbridge 578392, Regent Toss 578382; Curtains: Regent 665682; Chair cushions: Pimlico Plaid 647792

PAGE 130: Wallpaper: Farley Stripe 576610; Shower curtain, pillow, and shade: Bedford Cord 647651, piped in Bedford Cord 647659

PAGE 131: Wallpaper: Summer Fun 574961; Wallpaper border: Summer Fun 574971; Shower curtain: Kismet 658490, trimmed in Valley Plaid 600391; Valance and chair pad: Valley Plaid 600391

PAGES 132-133: Fabrics: Fredrik

663991; Wellington 665022; Windsor Washed Velvet 631562; Heritage 647066; Watermark 647635; Paint chips: Waverly (Norton & Son)

PAGE 136: Curtain (sheer): Miller 614830; Valance: La Petite Ferme 664675; Side chair: Checkpoint 647750; Pillow: Dominique 665562

PAGE 137: Waverly furniture (Lexington): Loose Back Sofa in Minicheck 647500; Tight Back Chair 7948-11 and Semi-attached Top Ottoman 7948-44 in Chantal 665771; Side chairs: Checkpoint 647750; Waverly Rug (Feizy): Rochelle 4267F2 Gold/Red; Pillows: Dominique 665562; Curtains (sheer): Miller 614830; Valances: La Petite Ferme 664675

PAGE 138: Pillow: Wellington 665022 with Windsor Washed Velvet trim 631561

PAGE 139: Sofa: Wellington 665022; Side chairs: Stockholm Stripe 647263; Ottoman: Windsor Washed Velvet 631562

PAGES 140-141: Roman shade: Zig Zag 647611; Pillows: Ming Garden 665321, Heritage 647065, Monroe Paisley 665311; Side chairs: Heritage 647065, Monroe Paisley 665311

PAGE 142: Pillows: Ming Garden 665321, Heritage 647065, Monroe Paisley 665311

PAGE 143: Chair: Monroe Paisley 665311; Pillow: Heritage 64706

PAGE 144: Curtains: Wetherburn 665252, Indienne 665232

PAGE 145: Waverly paint (Norton & Son): Clay WD182; Curtains and pillows: Wetherburn 665252, Indienne 665232; Seat cushion: Indienne 665232

PAGE 146: Wallpaper border: Ming Garden 576832; Wallpaper: Ming Garden Texture 576843; Chairs: Providence Check 647561; Window treatments: Ming Garden 665322, Heritage 647051, Providence Check 647561

PAGE 147: Wallpaper border: Calais 575630; Wallpaper: Calais 575640; Valance and chair: Lyon 664664; Sofa: Mini Check 647500; Pillows: La Petite Ferme 664675, Le Soleil 647463

PAGE 148: Waverly paint chips (Norton & Son); Fabrics: Duette White 614810; Le Soleil 647460; Perfection 647190; Zig Zag 647610; Capulet 647320; Bedford Cord 647650

PAGE 153: Curtains and slipcovers: Hot Spot 303350; Valance trim: Hot Spot 304662; Waverly rug: Mille Fleur WA106

PAGE 154: Tablecloth: Hot Spot 303350; Tablecloth topper and slipcovers: Oklahoma 370180; Waverly Rug (Beaulieu): Wedding 2416

PAGE 155: Slipcover: Oklahoma 370180; Pillow: Old World Linen 645603, Old World Linen 645600

PAGES 156-157: Sofa: Heritage 647050; Pillows: Zig Zag 647611, Zig Zag 647610, Old World Linen 645618; Waverly rug (Beaulieu): Palma Linen 3773

PAGES 158-159: Table runner: Silk Strie 664619; Tablecloth: Vintage Floral 665470

PAGES 160-161: Curtain: Duette 614810; Fabric panels and pillows: Old World Linen 645603, Old World Linen 645600; Comforter front: Capulet 647320; Comforter back: Zig Zag 647610; Bed skirt: Capulet 647320; Waverly upholstered armchair (Lexington) 565-883 covered in Hot Spot 303350; Waverly rug: WA107 Regent

PAGE 162: Wallpaper: Toulon 5500302; Tablecloth: Le Soleil 647461; Slipcovers: Vineyard Ticking 647684

PAGE 163: Wallpaper: Roswell Toss 5500480, Roswell Texture 5500490; Sofa: Heritage 647051; Pillow: Hot Spot 303390

Upholstery by Mark David Interiors, New York, NY; Designer Upholstery, Flushing, NY; and Girard's Decorating, Ridgewood, NJ; Fabrication by Melinda Combs, Leslie Meeker, and Claudia Larrabure.

index

index